WeightWatchers®

D0376050

suppers
& snacks

Roz Denny

SIMON & SCHUSTER

A VIACOM COMPANY

First published in Great Britain by Simon & Schuster, 1997
A Viacom Company

This edition produced for
The Book People Ltd
Hall Wood Avenue
Haydock
St Helens
WA11 9UL

First published 1997
Reprinted 2002

Simon & Schuster UK Ltd
Africa House
64–78 Kingsway
London WC2B 6AH

Design: Green Moore Lowenhoff
Cover design: Zoocity
Typesetting: Stylize
Photography: Steve Lee
Styling: Jo Harris
Food preparation: Wendy Lee

ISBN 0-68482-103-6

Printed in Hong Kong

Recipe notes:
Egg size is medium, unless otherwise stated.
Vegetables are medium-sized, unless otherwise stated.
It is very important to use proper measuring spoons, not cutlery, for spoon measures.
1 tablespoon = 15 ml; 1 teaspoon = 5 ml
Dried herbs can be substituted for fresh ones, but the flavour may not always
be as good. Halve the fresh-herb quantity stated in the recipe.

Contents

Introduction

The pace of our modern life seems to grow ever faster. We have less time to eat and less time to prepare food; instead of traditional home-cooked dishes we often choose quick-cook, convenience or take-away foods; instead of regular sit-down main meals, we eat more snacks and suppers.

But many convenience foods are high in saturated fat and Calories and, try as we might, we simply can't fit them into a healthy, low-fat diet.

That's where Weight Watchers comes in. Weight Watchers' new *1,2,3 Success*™ Programme doesn't place restrictions on the sort of meals you eat – if light meals and snacks suit your way of life, no problem. The *1,2,3 Success*™ Programme lets you eat the foods you really enjoy when you want them, and its Points system limits the amount of saturated fat in your diet. So without too much agonising you'll find yourself eating less saturated fat, fewer Calories.

If you do like the quick-and-easy approach to cooking, you'll find that meat is an excellent basis for healthy meals. Some of our old favourites – such as lean chops and steaks – have always been speedy to prepare, but next time you pass the chiller cabinets of a well-stocked supermarket or take a look in the window of your local butcher, you'll find many wonderful new ideas: lean stir-fry strips that can be tipped straight from the pack into the pan; trimmed cubed meat ready for casseroles or kebabs; and boned and rolled joints that need no extra preparation before going into the oven, and are very easy to carve.

Meat has become leaner over the years; lean, trimmed cuts of beef, lamb and pork are now readily available, and there are leaner, reduced-fat varieties of mince and sausages which have much less fat than the traditional varieties and which can easily fit into a low-fat diet.

As well as being low in fat, lean meat is high in protein and a valuable source of iron. It's important to make sure that you're getting enough iron – anaemia is one of the most common deficiency diseases in the UK. Iron is essential for forming healthy red blood cells. Children especially need good amounts of iron as do young women preparing for a family. Other useful nutrients in lean meat include zinc (needed for growth, healing and a healthy immune system) and vitamins of the B group (essential for metabolic reactions in the body).

Weight Watchers recommend that you eat a variety of different foods. Meat, which is packed with nutrients, goes brilliantly with starchy foods like potatoes, rice, pasta or bread, as well as vitamin-rich vegetables and salads.

Keep the fat levels low when you cook meat. This is easily done by grilling, baking or dry-frying meat instead of shallow or deep-frying. Avoid high-fat pastry toppings and crumb coatings and add the minimum amount of fat or oil you can get away with. Use low-fat yogurt, fromage frais or half-fat crème fraîche instead of cream.

There are plenty of good reasons to eat lean meat; and now we know we can include it in our diet without adversely affecting our waistlines. Great news for those of us who appreciate the great tastes of beef, pork and lamb.

Meat for One

Meat makes an ideal basis for healthy meals for one. All too often when we're just cooking for ourselves the temptation is to fall back on convenience foods – the trouble is they're often high in Points and Calories.

The cuts of meat available now are quick to prepare and they're packed with nutrients – you can eat fast and healthily. From simple sandwiches to hot, cooked dishes, such as stir-fries and kebabs, there are some good meaty meal ideas here.

Quick Curried Mince Pilaff

A tasty, all-in-one supper. Serve with a salad of grated raw carrot dressed with a little fresh lemon juice and a sprinkling of poppy seeds.

Serves: 1
Preparation and cooking time: 20 minutes
Freezing: not recommended
Points per serving: with beef 6; with lamb 7; with pork 6
Calories per serving: with beef 545; with lamb 565; with pork 530

¹/₄ small onion or 1 shallot, chopped
¹/₄ small green pepper, chopped

1 garlic clove, crushed, or 1 teaspoon garlic purée
1 teaspoon sunflower oil
105 g (3¹/₂ oz) extra-lean minced beef, or minced lamb or pork
2 teaspoons mild curry powder
75 g (2¹/₂ oz) basmati rice
300 ml (¹/₂ pint) stock or water
2 teaspoons mango chutney
salt and freshly ground black pepper

❶ Heat a heavy-based frying-pan until quite hot, then add the onion, pepper, garlic, oil and 2 tablespoons of water. Stir, cover and cook gently for 5 minutes until softened.

❷ Uncover the frying-pan and raise the heat. Stir in the mince, heating until browned and crumbly.

❸ Stir in the curry powder and rice. Cook for 1 minute and then mix in the stock or water, chutney

and seasoning. Bring to the boil, cover and simmer gently for 10 minutes.

❹ Remove the frying-pan from the heat and leave to stand, still covered, for another 5 minutes. Then uncover, fluff with a fork, and check the seasoning.

Quick Curried Mince Pilaff

Chinese Lamb Stir-Fry

Lamb is a delicious meat to use in Chinese cooking, as its slightly sweet flavour is complemented so well by soy sauce and sesame oil. Ideally, use lamb stir-fry strips, or you could buy a lean, boneless leg steak and slice it up. This is a really easy all-in-one meal!

Serves: 1

Preparation and cooking time: 20 minutes

Freezing: not recommended

Points per serving: with stir-fry strips $7^1/_2$;
with leg steak $6^1/_2$

Calories per serving: with stir-fry strips 495;
with leg steak 470

60 g (2 oz) quick-cooking spaghetti
90 g (3 oz) lamb stir-fry strips or boneless leg steak, trimmed of all fat and cut in thin strips

1 teaspoon sunflower oil
$^1/_4$ small red pepper, sliced thinly
2 salad onions, sliced
1 carrot, cut in thin sticks
1 small courgette, cut in thin sticks
1 tablespoon dry sherry or vermouth (optional)
2 tablespoons light soy sauce
1 teaspoon sesame oil
1 teaspoon sesame seeds
freshly ground black pepper

❶ Break the spaghetti in half and cook according to the packet instructions. Drain, rinse in cold water and set aside.

❷ Heat a non-stick wok or heavy-based frying-pan until quite hot and then stir-fry the lamb strips for about 2 minutes until browned. Remove the lamb and keep warm.

❸ Add the oil to the wok and heat again until quite hot. Add the vegetables and stir-fry for about 2 minutes until just softened. Return the lamb to the wok.

❹ Mix in the sherry or vermouth (if using), soy sauce and sesame oil. Heat well until bubbling, then stir in the spaghetti. Reheat and check the seasoning, then sprinkle over the sesame seeds and serve immediately.

To help cut down on fat when cooking meat, preheat an empty non-stick frying-pan until you can feel a good steady heat rising. Then add the meat and stir it frequently. You will find the meat browns attractively without sticking.

Honey-Mustard Pork with Bubble-and-Squeak Mash

A chunky pork chop makes a delicious meal for one person. Combine your vegetables in a tasty and traditional way with a bubble-and-squeak mash. A lean lamb steak, trimmed of all fat, can be used instead of pork. If there is still a little fat on your chop when you grill it, do be sure to cut it off before you eat it!

Serves: 1

Preparation and cooking time: 25 minutes

Freezing: not recommended

Points per serving: with pork 6½; with lamb 7

Calories per serving: with pork 425; with lamb 430

210 g (7 oz) potatoes, peeled and diced

1 teaspoon low-fat spread

1 tablespoon skimmed milk

a little grated nutmeg

105 g (3½ oz) green cabbage, shredded

1 salad onion, chopped

150 g (5 oz) pork chop, trimmed of all fat

a pinch of dried thyme

1 teaspoon coarse-grain mustard

1 teaspoon clear honey

1 teaspoon lemon juice

salt and freshly ground black pepper

❶ Boil the potatoes in lightly salted water until tender, about 15 minutes, then drain, reserving the water. Mash the potatoes until smooth with the low-fat spread and milk. Season well, adding nutmeg to taste. Set aside.

❷ Boil the cabbage in the reserved potato water for about 5 minutes, then drain well and mix into the potato along with the salad onion.

❸ Meanwhile, preheat the grill and, when hot, cook the pork chop for about 3 minutes on each side until just cooked. Mix the thyme, mustard and honey together and spread on both sides. Grill on each side for a further 2 minutes until golden brown and bubbling.

❹ Serve the bubble-and-squeak mash on a warmed plate with the pork chop. Drizzle the lemon juice over the chop just before serving.

Dab grilled and dry-fried meat with kitchen paper to remove fat from meat after cooking.

Honey-Mustard Pork with Bubble-and-Squeak Mash

Bacon and Spinach Salad

Now that spinach is sold washed and ready to eat, it has become very popular in quick-and-easy dishes.
In this nutritious salad it is tossed with crispy bacon and low-fat croûtons.

Serves: 1
Preparation and cooking time: 15 minutes
Freezing: not recommended
Points per serving: 3
Calories per serving: 160

1 slice wholemeal bread, crusts removed
1 garlic clove, halved

90 g (3 oz) young spinach leaves, trimmed of thick stalks
60 g (2 oz) button mushrooms, sliced
1 tablespoon low-calorie French dressing
2 lean back-bacon rashers, rind removed and cut in thin strips
1 tablespoon balsamic or red wine vinegar
salt and freshly ground black pepper

❶ Toast the bread under a low grill until it is crisp. Then remove from the heat and rub both sides with the cut halves of garlic. Cut the toast into small croûtons. Set aside.

❷ Mix the spinach and mushrooms in a small salad bowl, season well and toss in the dressing.

❸ Preheat a small non-stick frying-pan until quite hot. Dry-fry the bacon strips for about 2 minutes until crisp. Stir in the vinegar and then toss immediately into the spinach and mushroom salad. Sprinkle over the croûtons and serve immediately.

Pasta Neapolitan

There is something very comforting about a plate of pasta and sauce. This dish only uses a small amount of mince
so freeze what you have left over to use another time. The anchovy essence livens up the dish without tasting at all
fishy – well worth trying as a flavouring with meat.

Serves: 1
Preparation and cooking time: 25 minutes
Freezing: not recommended
Points per serving: with beef 5$\frac{1}{2}$; with lamb 6$\frac{1}{2}$; with pork 5$\frac{1}{2}$
Calories per serving: with beef 455; with lamb 475; with pork 450

60 g (2 oz) pasta shapes
90 g (3 oz) extra-lean minced beef, or minced lamb or pork

$\frac{1}{2}$ small onion, chopped
$\frac{1}{4}$ small green, red or yellow pepper, chopped
200 g can chopped tomatoes
1 tablespoon tomato purée
$\frac{1}{2}$ teaspoon dried oregano or mixed herbs
2 teaspoons anchovy essence (optional)
1 tablespoon half-fat crème fraîche
salt and freshly ground black pepper

1 Cook the pasta according to the packet instructions. Drain and set aside.

2 Meanwhile heat a non-stick frying-pan until quite hot. Dry-fry the mince, stirring often until lightly browned and crumbly, about 3 minutes.

3 Stir in the onion and pepper and cook for another 3 minutes until softened. Add the tomatoes, tomato purée, herbs, anchovy essence (if using) and seasoning. Bring to the boil, then simmer for 5 minutes, stirring once or twice.

4 Toss in the pasta and crème fraîche and reheat until very hot. Serve immediately.

Ham Coleslaw Sandwich

Home-made coleslaw goes so well with lean, smoked ham. Serve them together on a slice of fresh rye or wholemeal, crusty bread (so you don't need to 'butter' it) for a healthy and quick meal.

Serves: 1
Preparation time: 10 minutes
Freezing: not recommended
Points per serving: 4
Calories per serving: 205

3 tablespoons white cabbage, shredded thinly
1 medium carrot, grated coarsely
1 small stick celery, sliced thinly

1 tablespoon chopped green or red pepper
1 small salad onion, chopped finely
1 tablespoon low-calorie mayonnaise
2 teaspoons low-fat natural yogurt
1 slice crusty rye or wholemeal bread
1 lettuce leaf
45 g (1¹/₂ oz) lean ham, sliced thinly or wafer-sliced
salt and freshly ground black pepper
cherry tomatoes or radishes, sliced, to garnish

1 To make the coleslaw, mix the cabbage, carrot, celery, pepper and salad onion together. Season well and then mix in the mayonnaise and yogurt.

2 Put the bread on a plate, top with the lettuce leaf, spoon over the coleslaw and then arrange the ham on top, folding if necessary. Grind some extra black pepper on top.

3 Garnish with the tomato or radish slices and sprinkle with the cress.

Steak Sandwich

You won't need to use any butter for this quick, tasty snack. Choose fresh crusty bread and trickle over any pan juices from the steak before you put the meat between the bread.

Serves: 1

Preparation and cooking time: 10 minutes

Freezing: not recommended

Points per serving: with sirloin 5; with rump 4½

Calories per serving: with sirloin 330; with rump 325

75 g (2½ oz) piece of crusty french bread

low-fat cooking spray

75 g (2½ oz) sirloin or rump steak, trimmed of all fat and cut in thin strips

¼ **small onion or 1 shallot, sliced thinly**

1–2 teaspoons coarse-grain mustard

2 lettuce leaves

1 small tomato, sliced thinly

salt and freshly ground black pepper

❶ Slit the bread in half lengthways and set aside.

❷ Heat a small non-stick frying-pan until you can feel a good heat rising. Spray lightly with the cooking spray, then add the steak.

❸ Stir-fry quickly for about 2 minutes. Remove, season well and place in the bread.

❹ Spray the pan once more with the cooking spray and add the sliced onion or shallot. Cook, stirring occasionally, for about 3 minutes until just softened. Spoon on top of the steak.

❺ Spoon over the mustard. Season well, add the lettuce and tomato. Trickle over any pan juices and sandwich the bread halves together. Eat while still warm.

Lamb Kebab with Peppers and Mushrooms

Tender, lean lamb steak is ideal as a quick meal for one. Cube the meat and vegetables and skewer them together on a satay stick. Serve with plain boiled rice or pitta bread and a crisp green salad. Boneless pork steak could be used instead.

Serves: 1
Preparation and cooking time: 20 minutes
Freezing: not recommended
Points per serving: with lamb 2; with pork 2
Calories per serving: with lamb 140; with pork 135

90 g (3 oz) boneless lamb steak, trimmed of all fat
a good pinch of garlic salt
¹/₂ teaspoon dried rosemary, crushed
2 button mushrooms, trimmed
¹/₂ small courgette, cut in 3 chunks
¹/₄ small red pepper, cut in 3 chunks
low-fat cooking spray
freshly ground black pepper

❶ Cut the lamb steak into 2.5 cm (1-inch) cubes. Sprinkle with the garlic salt and crushed rosemary.

❷ On a metal skewer or long wooden satay stick, alternate the cubes of meat with the vegetables. Season with pepper.

❸ Preheat the grill until hot and spray the kebab lightly with the cooking spray. Cook for about 5 minutes on each side until the meat is just cooked and still juicy.

Bacon and Spinach Salad (page 12)
Lamb Kebab with Peppers and Mushrooms

Quick Meals

Meals in minutes may sound too good to be true if we're looking for dishes that are more than just snacks, but if lean meat forms the core of the recipe, you will be amazed at the great variety of exciting ideas you can just 'rustle up'. There are plenty of lean, quick-cook cuts available now that suit home-made fast-food recipes: lean minces, stir-fry strips, pan-fry steaks and chops. Beef, pork and lamb cuts can all be used to give new flavours to well-loved family favourites.

Pork and Leek Stir-Fry

Lean pork tenderloin only needs to be sliced and then stir-fried with vegetables for a quick, easy meal. Serve with tangy orange and soy sauce, and some sesame rice and you have a great, tasty supper.

Serves: 4
Preparation and cooking time: 20 minutes
Freezing: not recommended
Points per serving: 6½
Total Points per recipe: 26
Calories per serving: 415

210 g (7 oz) long-grain rice
2 teaspoons sesame oil
1 tablespoon sesame seeds
420 g (14 oz) pork tenderloin, trimmed of all fat
  and sliced thinly

1 tablespoon sunflower oil
1 red pepper, de-seeded and sliced thinly
2 medium leeks, sliced thinly
2 garlic cloves, crushed or 2 teaspoons
  garlic purée
2 tablespoons dry vermouth or sherry (optional)
juice of 1 medium orange
3 tablespoons dark soy sauce
salt and freshly ground black pepper

❶ Cook the rice according to the packet instructions. Drain, season and toss in the sesame oil and sesame seeds. Set aside and keep warm.

❷ For the stir-fry, heat a non-stick wok or large non-stick frying-pan. When the pan is quite hot, brown the pork slices for 2–3 minutes.

❸ Remove, add the oil and then stir-fry the pepper, leeks and garlic for a minute or two. Stir in 3

tablespoons of water, cover and cook over a medium heat for 3 minutes, shaking the pan once or twice.

❹ Return the meat to the pan and add the vermouth or sherry (if using). Cook for 1 minute, then stir in the orange juice, soy sauce and seasoning. Simmer for another 2 minutes. Serve immediately with the rice.

Ham with Creamy Herb Tagliatelle

Pasta is always popular. This dish is deliciously creamy without being high in fat.

Serves: 2
Preparation and cooking time: 20 minutes
Freezing: not recommended
Points per serving: 6
Total Points per recipe: 12
Calories per serving: 330

105 g (3¹/₂ oz) tagliatelle
105 g (3¹/₂ oz) lean ham, cut in thin strips

3 salad onions, sliced
2 teaspoons olive or sunflower oil
105 g (3¹/₂ oz) young spinach leaves, chopped
¹/₂ teaspoon dried mixed herbs
150 ml (¹/₄ pint) stock
2 tablespoons half-fat crème fraîche
salt, freshly ground black pepper and grated
nutmeg

❶ Boil the tagliatelle according to the packet instructions. Drain, rinse in cold water and set aside.
❷ Stir-fry the ham and onions in the oil for about 2 minutes until just cooked. Then toss in the spinach, stirring until wilted.

❸ Add the herbs, pour in the stock and bubble for about another minute. Finally mix in the crème fraîche, season well with salt and pepper and add the grated nutmeg to taste.
❹ Toss in the tagliatelle, mixing well and serve immediately.

Creamy Steak and Onions with Baked Potatoes

If you like beef stroganoff, then you'll love this low-fat version served as a baked potato filling. This is an ideal quick and tasty meal if you microwave the potatoes.

Serves: 4
Preparation time: 15 minutes + 1 hour cooking or 10–15 minutes microwaving
Freezing: not recommended
Points per serving: 4
Total Points per recipe: 16
Calories per serving: with rump 325; with sirloin 330

4 baking potatoes about 150 g (5 oz) each, scrubbed and scored

1 tablespoon olive or sunflower oil
210 g (7 oz) rump or sirloin steak, trimmed of all fat and cut in thin strips
1 onion, sliced thinly
150 g (5 oz) mushrooms, sliced
2 garlic cloves, crushed or 1 teaspoon garlic purée
¹/₂ teaspoon dried tarragon
3 tablespoons half-fat crème fraîche
2 tablespoons chopped fresh parsley (optional)
salt and freshly ground black pepper

❶ Bake the potatoes. If using an oven, cook for 1 hour at Gas Mark 5/190°C/375°F, or in a microwave for 10–15 minutes, depending on the power of your oven. (Check the manufacturer's instructions.)
❷ For the filling, heat the oil in a medium frying-pan and stir-fry the steak and onion for 2–3 minutes.

Add the mushrooms, garlic or garlic purée, and tarragon and cook for another 2 minutes.
❸ Season well, then stir in the crème fraîche and parsley (if using). Slit the potatoes in half and spoon in the filling.

Chop Suey with Noodles

Chop suey is a Chinese-inspired American dish, so called because all the vegetables are chopped up! Stir-fry strips of beef, pork or lamb can be used and the dish can be served alongside the noodles, or tossed with them. Prepare all the vegetables and sauce first so the meat is freshly cooked.

Serves: 4

Preparation and cooking time: 20 minutes

Freezing: not recommended

Points per serving: with beef 6; with lamb 7; with pork 5½

Total Points per recipe: with beef 24; with lamb 28; with pork 22

Calories per serving: with beef 430; with lamb 455; with pork 420

210 g (7 oz) egg thread noodles
1 tablespoon sunflower oil
420 g (14 oz) stir-fry strips of beef, lamb or pork, trimmed of all fat

2 carrots, cut in thin sticks
4 salad onions, sliced
150 g (5 oz) bean shoots
1 red or yellow pepper
150 g (5 oz) whole green beans, topped and tailed, then halved
2 garlic cloves, crushed or 2 teaspoons garlic purée
1 tablespoon ginger purée (optional)
150 ml (¼ pint) stock
2 teaspoons cornflour
3 tablespoons dark soy sauce
2 tablespoons tomato ketchup
freshly ground black pepper

1 Cook the noodles according to the packet instructions and then drain and set aside.

2 Heat a wok or large frying-pan and when hot add the oil and stir-fry the meat strips for about 2 minutes, tossing until lightly browned and cooked

3 Remove the meat strips with a slotted spoon and set aside. Add the vegetables, garlic and ginger

(if using) plus 4 tablespoons of the stock. Stir-fry for 5 minutes, tossing until the vegetables are softened.

4 Return the meat to the pan. Mix together the remaining stock with the cornflour, soy sauce and ketchup and add to the wok. Season with pepper. Either toss the noodles into the wok or serve them separately with the chop suey.

Pork and Bacon Paella

For an authentic texture, use risotto rice which will give the dish a wonderful creaminess without adding any Points or Calories. A true paella is shaken during cooking, not stirred, so the rice grains remain plump and whole!

Serves: 4
Preparation and cooking time: 30 minutes
Freezing: not recommended
Points per serving: 5
Total Points per recipe: 20
Calories per serving: 340

3 lean back-bacon rashers, rind removed and
    trimmed
210 g (7 oz) pork tenderloin, boneless steaks or
    cubed pork, trimmed of all fat
1 medium onion, chopped

2 garlic cloves, crushed or 2 teaspoons garlic purée
1 teaspoon dried thyme
1/2 green pepper, chopped
3 tomatoes, skinned and chopped
210 g (7 oz) risotto rice or long-grain rice, but not
    easy-cook
1 tablespoon ground paprika
1/2 teaspoon ground turmeric
900 ml (11/2 pints) stock
1 large bay leaf
120 g (4 oz) frozen broad beans
salt and freshly ground black pepper

❶ Cut the bacon into small pieces. If using tenderloin or steaks, cut these into small pieces. Heat a large heavy-based frying-pan until quite hot, then dry-fry the two meats until lightly browned. Remove and keep warm.

❷ Add 2 tablespoons of water to the pan juices and stir in the onion, garlic, thyme, pepper and tomatoes. Sauté for 5 minutes, stirring the pan occasionally until the vegetables have softened.

❸ Stir in the rice and spices and cook for a minute. Return the meat to the pan and mix in the stock, bay leaf, broad beans and seasoning.

❹ Bring to the boil, stirring once, then cover the pan and simmer for about 15 minutes, shaking the pan occasionally, but do not lift the lid. As with all rices dishes, allow the paella to stand in the pan for 5 minutes before serving – this helps to separate the grains.

Creamy Steak and Onions with Baked Potatoes (page 20)
Pork and Bacon Paella

Lamb with Ratatouille and New Potatoes

Juicy, tender British lamb is a natural partner for the punchy flavours of ratatouille vegetables. If you prefer, you could make the ratatouille mixture ahead of time and then simply grill the lamb before eating. The vegetable mixture could even be frozen ahead in bulk (you can re-heat it straight from the freezer). If there is still a little fat on your chop when you grill it, do be sure to cut it off before you eat it!

Serves: 2
Preparation and cooking time: 30 minutes
Freezing: recommended
Points per serving: 5
Total Points per recipe: 10
Calories per serving: 300

210 g (7 oz) new potatoes, scrubbed
2 teaspoons olive oil, preferably extra virgin
1 small onion, sliced

2 garlic cloves, crushed or 2 teaspoons garlic
    purée
1/2 medium aubergine, cut in chunks
1 courgette, cut in chunks
1/2 yellow or red pepper, sliced
200 g can chopped tomatoes
1 teaspoon dried mixed herbs
2 × 120 g (4 oz) lamb chump chops, trimmed of
    all fat
salt and freshly ground black pepper

❶ Boil the potatoes in lightly salted water until just tender, about 15 minutes. Drain and set aside.

❷ In a medium-sized saucepan, heat the oil until quite hot and then stir in the onion, garlic, aubergine, courgette and pepper. When well coated with the oil, add 4 tablespoons of water plus salt and pepper. Cover and cook gently for 5 minutes until softened, shaking the pan occasionally.

❸ Stir in the canned tomatoes, herbs, potatoes and seasoning. Return to a simmer and cook, uncovered, for 10 minutes. Check the seasoning and set aside.

❹ Meanwhile, preheat the grill until hot. Season the lamb and grill for about 5 minutes on each side or according to your liking. If you like your lamb well done, then allow 7–8 minutes each side.

❺ Spoon the ratatouille on to plates and serve with the lamb.

The grilling times for steaks depend upon the type and thickness of the meat. For beef steaks 2–3 cm (3/4–1 1/4 inches) thick allow 2 1/2–3 minutes each side for a rare steak, 4–5 minutes each side for a medium steak and 6–7 minutes each side for a well-done steak. For a double-loin or leg lamb steak 2 cm (3/4–inch) thick allow 6–8 minutes each side.

Bacon Chops with Lemon Glaze and Apricot Rice (page 27)
Lamb with Ratatouille and New Potatoes

All-in-one Mince and Tatties

A glorious winter warmer, this makes a wonderful supper dish to eat curled up in front of the TV or the fire. Vary the vegetables if you like. Serve with some lightly-boiled hot, crisp greens such as cabbage or brussels sprouts.

Serves: 4
Preparation and cooking time: 30 minutes
Freezing: recommended
Points per serving: with beef 6$^1/_2$; with pork 6; with lamb 7$^1/_2$
Total Points per recipe: with beef 26; with pork 24; with lamb 30
Calories per serving: with beef 350; with pork 340; with lamb 380

480 g (1 lb) extra-lean minced beef, or minced pork or lamb

480 g (1 lb) potatoes, scrubbed and chopped into small dice
1 celery stick, sliced
2 carrots, grated coarsely
$^1/_2$ small swede, or 2 turnips, peeled and chopped
2 garlic cloves, crushed or 1 teaspoon garlic purée
6 tablespoons stale ale or dry cider (optional)
2 tablespoons flour
600 ml (1 pint) beef stock
1 teaspoon dried thyme
salt and freshly ground black pepper

❶ Heat a wok or large frying-pan until quite hot, then dry-fry the mince, stirring frequently until browned and crumbly.

❷ Add all the vegetables and the garlic and fry for about 5 minutes then stir in the ale or cider (if using) and cook until evaporated. Mix in the flour.

❸ Pour in the stock and stir in the thyme and seasoning. Bring to the boil, then lower the heat to a simmer and cook, uncovered, for about 15 minutes, stirring occasionally.

Mexican Mince Salad

Toss spiced mince into crisp lettuce for an exciting and quick main-meal salad. Treat yourself to a few tortilla chips too!

Serves: 2
Preparation and cooking time: 20 minutes
Freezing: not recommended
Points per serving: with pork 6; with beef 6$^1/_2$
Total Points per recipe: with pork 12; with beef 13
Calories per serving: with pork 410; with beef 415

$^1/_4$ iceberg lettuce, shredded
2 salad onions, sliced
$^1/_4$ green pepper, sliced thinly
2 tomatoes, chopped in chunks
1 carrot, grated coarsely
30 g (1 oz) tortilla chips

For the spicy mince:
210 g (7 oz) extra-lean minced beef or minced pork
1 garlic clove, crushed or 1 teaspoon garlic purée
1–2 teaspoons mild chilli powder, according to taste
$^1/_2$ teaspoon ground cumin
1 tablespoon tomato purée
200 g can red kidney beans, drained
1 tablespoon barbecue or mild chilli relish
salt and freshly ground black pepper

① First, prepare the salad. Toss the shredded lettuce in a bowl with the onions, green pepper, tomatoes and carrot. Season lightly and chill.

② Heat a non-stick frying-pan until quite hot and dry-fry the mince for about 3 minutes, stirring well to break up the lumps.

③ Add the garlic and spices and cook for 1 minute. Mix in the tomato purée, kidney beans and chilli relish. Season well and cook for another minute or two.

④ Toss into the salad and mix in the tortilla chips. Serve immediately so you can appreciate the contrast of temperatures, textures and flavours!

Bacon Chops with Lemon Glaze and Apricot Rice

British bacon chops make an excellent supper dish and take almost no time to cook. They come lean and boneless and may only need a little extra trimming to remove any remaining fat. Their mild, salty flavour goes well with this fruity rice. Serve with a crisp salad.

Serves: 2
Preparation and cooking time: 30 minutes
Freezing: not recommended
Points per serving: 5½
Total Points per recipe: 11
Calories per serving: 365

105 g (3½ oz) easy-cook basmati rice
2 spring onions, chopped

6 no-soak apricots, snipped
300 ml (½ pint) stock
1 teaspoon low-fat spread
2 × 75 g (2½ oz) bacon chops, trimmed of all fat
juice of 1 small lemon
a good pinch of dried sage
1 teaspoon honey
1 teaspoon garlic purée (optional)
salt and freshly ground black pepper

① First, cook the apricot rice: put the rice, spring onions, apricots, stock and some seasoning into a medium-size saucepan. Bring to the boil, then cover and simmer gently for 15 minutes without lifting the lid.

② Remove from the heat and leave to stand without lifting the lid. After 5 minutes, fluff with a fork and mix in the low-fat spread. Set aside.

③ Heat a medium-size non-stick frying-pan until quite hot, then dry-fry the bacon chops for about 5 minutes on each side. Stir in the lemon juice, sage, honey and garlic purée (if using). Season with the freshly ground black pepper and serve with the rice.

Texan Burgers

Use extra-lean mince to make your own burgers. You can add some exciting flavours, such as these Tex-Mex-style spices.
Serve with some salad and fresh burger buns. Don't forget the tomato ketchup and mustard!

Serves: 2
Preparation and cooking time: 12–15 minutes
Freezing: not recommended
Points per serving: with beef 6¹/₂; with pork 6;
  with lamb 7¹/₂
Total Points per recipe: with beef 13; with pork 12;
  with lamb 15
Calories per serving: with beef 385; with pork 375;
  with lamb 410

1 small onion
240 g (8 oz) extra-lean minced beef, minced pork
  or lamb

1 teaspoon salt
1 teaspoon dried oregano
1 teaspoon mild chilli powder
¹/₂ teaspoon ground cumin
freshly ground black pepper
To serve:
2 fresh burger buns, split in half
4 lettuce leaves
2 tomatoes, sliced thinly
mustard
ketchup

❶ Take the onion and slice one half thinly. Grate the other half.
❷ Mix the mince with the salt, oregano, spices, grated onion and freshly ground black pepper. When thoroughly blended, shape into four burgers.
❸ Prepare the buns, allowing one half per burger. Place a lettuce leaf and some tomato slices on each.
❹ Preheat the grill until hot. Cook the burgers for about 5–6 minutes on each side or until cooked through.
❺ Place the burger on top of the tomato and lettuce, season lightly and serve with the mustard, ketchup and onion rings.

Beefy Watercress and Potato Salad

This is a good way to make two servings from one juicy steak. It also makes a nice light supper on a warm summer
evening. Use sea-salt for the best flavour.

Serves: 2
Preparation and cooking time: 25 minutes
Freezing: not recommended
Points per serving: with sirloin 5¹/₂; with rump 5¹/₂
Total Points per recipe: with sirloin 11; with
  rump 11
Calories per serving: with sirloin 360; with
  rump 350

2 eggs
240 g (8 oz) baby new potatoes

low-fat cooking spray
240 g (8 oz) sirloin or rump steak, trimmed
  of all fat
10 cm (4-inch) cucumber, halved lengthways
1 bunch or pack of watercress, trimmed of thick
  stalks
2 tablespoons oil-free French dressing
2 teaspoons coarse-grain mustard
salt and freshly ground black pepper
a few leaves of lettuce, to serve (e.g. Oak Leaf,
  Frisée or round)

Mexican Mince Salad (page 26)
Texan Burgers

28

1 Hard boil the eggs, and then cool and peel. Cut in quarters and set aside.

2 Halve the potatoes and boil until tender – about 15 minutes – then drain. Season and leave to cool.

3 Preheat a heavy-based frying-pan or ridged grill pan and spray lightly with cooking spray. Cook the steak. For a rare steak allow about 5 minutes, for medium 8 minutes and for well-done about 10 minutes, turning half-way through the cooking time. Remove the steak and set aside.

4 Using a teaspoon, remove the seeds from the cucumber halves then slice into thin crescents. Mix with the watercress and cooled potatoes.

5 Whisk the dressing with the mustard and 1 tablespoon of water. Toss with the watercress, cucumber and potato.

6 Now slice the steak thinly, season well and toss into the salad along with any meaty juices. Carefully mix in the egg quarters. Serve immediately at room temperature on two plates lined with lettuce leaves.

Chipolata and Mushroom Kebabs

Chipolata sausages can easily be included in your healthy diet. Choose lower-fat varieties and grill them rather than fry. Serve these colourful kebabs with wholemeal pittas, crisp lettuce and a tangy yogurt dressing.

Serves: 2
Preparation and cooking time: 20 minutes
Freezing: not recommended
Points per serving: 5
Total Points per recipe: 10
Calories per serving: 385

6 low-fat chipolata sausages
1 small onion, quartered and separated into
   segments
1/2 red or yellow pepper, cut into 6 chunks

6 button mushrooms, trimmed of stalks
low-fat cooking spray
2 medium wholemeal pittas
For the salad:
iceberg lettuce
3 tablespoons low-fat natural yogurt
juice of 1/2 lemon
1/4 teaspoon garlic salt
1 tablespoon chopped fresh parsley or dill or
   1/2 teaspoon dried mixed herbs
salt and freshly ground black pepper

1 Bend the chipolata sausages into a squashed 'C' shape. Stick the sausages, onion, pepper and mushrooms on to two wooden or metal skewers, alternating the different ingredients. Season well and spray lightly with the cooking spray.

2 Preheat the grill and when it reaches an even heat, grill the kebabs for about 5–7 minutes on each side, taking care not to let the sausages burn. While the kebabs are being grilled, pop the pittas under the grill to warm through.

3 Meanwhile, prepare the salad. Shred the lettuce allowing a good handful per serving. Mix the yogurt with the lemon, garlic salt, herbs and seasoning.

4 To serve, stuff the pittas with the lettuce. Push the chipolatas and vegetables off the sticks or skewers and add these to the pittas. Spoon in the dressing. Eat with your fingers.

Beefy Watercress and Potato Salad (page 28)
Chipolata and Mushroom Kebabs

Family Meals

Although many families no longer sit down together every day for a main meal, providing good wholesome food is just as much a priority as it ever was. Meat requires very little preparation (which is ideal for hard-pressed family cooks), and roasting is one of the easiest methods of cooking there is. You can add simple, quick flavourings in the form of marinades or herbs and easily create some really memorable dishes. Even slow-cooking cuts, such as braising steak, need very little preparation and can be left alone to cook. There's no need for family-style meals to be high in Calories and Points. Simply choose well-trimmed meat, add some potatoes, pasta or rice and some lightly cooked vegetables, and you have a meal that can easily fit into a healthy, low-fat diet.

Chinese Marinated Lamb

Marinades suit the new boneless joints of meats which are ready-rolled for roasting. This marinade gives a delicious barbecue tang, ideally suited to lamb, but it would work equally well with pork. Serve with a light stir-fry of vegetables and some egg noodles or with boiled Thai or basmati rice. If there is still a little fat on your joint when you roast it, do be sure to cut it off at the table!

Serves: 8
Preparation time: 10 minutes + marinating + 2 hours cooking
Freezing: recommended
Points per serving: 6¹/₂
Total Points per recipe: 52
Calories per serving: 250

1 boned and rolled leg of lean lamb, about
   1.25 kg (3 lb) weight
1 tablespoon sunflower oil
1 small onion, grated

2 garlic cloves, crushed or 2 teaspoons garlic
   purée
1 teaspoon ginger purée
3 tablespoons dark soy sauce
2 tablespoons tomato ketchup
1 tablespoon Worcestershire sauce
1 tablespoon dry sherry (optional)
2 teaspoons clear honey
1 teaspoon five-spice powder
freshly ground black pepper
watercress sprigs, to garnish

1 Trim the lamb of any fat and pierce it several times with a metal skewer. Place it in a polythene bag.

2 Mix all the remaining ingredients (except the watercress) in a jug, whisking until smooth, then pour into the bag and rub well into the lamb. Seal tightly and chill overnight in the fridge.

3 Preheat the oven to Gas Mark 4/180°C/350°F. Remove the meat from the bag and place on a rack in a small ovenproof dish. Roast for up to 2 hours (see Cook's note) until tender, basting occasionally with any leftover marinade.

4 Allow the joint to stand for 10 minutes before carving it into thin slices. Reserve the roasting juices and pour them over the slices as you serve them. Serve garnished with watercress sprigs.

Cook's note: When cooking lamb, for medium-cooked meat allow 25 minutes per 480 g (1 lb) plus 25 minutes; for well-done meat allow 30 minutes per 480 g (1 lb) plus 30 minutes.

Thai-Style Pot Roast Pork (page 38)
Chinese Marinated Lamb

Country Cottage Pie

A cottage pie is a favourite family supper. This one has a nice selection of vegetables with it too. You can vary the recipe by using any of the lean minces. A bowl of hot steaming peas is perfect with this dish (remember to add the Points).

Serves: 4

Preparation time: 20 minutes + 30 minutes cooking

Freezing: recommended

Points per serving: with beef 8; with pork 7$^1/_2$; with lamb 8$^1/_2$

Total Points per recipe: with beef 32; with pork 30; with lamb 34

Calories per serving: with beef 445; with pork 435; with lamb 475

720 g (1$^1/_2$ lb) potatoes, peeled and chopped
2 teaspoons low-fat spread
4–6 tablespoons skimmed milk
$^1/_4$ teaspoon ground nutmeg
480 g (1 lb) extra-lean minced beef, or minced pork or lamb

2 leeks, washed and chopped
2 carrots, grated coarsely
1 celery stick, chopped finely
1 small green or yellow pepper, de-seeded and chopped
120 g (4 oz) mushrooms, chopped
1 teaspoon dried mixed herbs
2 tablespoons flour
240 ml (8 fl oz) stock or water
2 tablespoons soy sauce
1 tablespoon Worcestershire sauce
2 tablespoons dried breadcrumbs
salt and freshly ground black pepper

❶ Boil the potatoes in lightly salted water until tender, about 15 minutes, then drain. Return to the heat for a minute or two to dry off, and then add the low-fat spread and milk. Mash until smooth and beat in the nutmeg and seasoning. Set aside.

❷ Meanwhile, preheat the oven to Gas Mark 6/200°C/400°F. Heat a large non-stick frying-pan until really hot and dry-fry the mince until browned and crumbly. Stir to break up any lumps.

❸ Add the leeks, carrots, celery, pepper and mushrooms and cook in the pan juices for 5 minutes, stirring occasionally.

❹ Mix in the herbs and flour, and cook for 1 minute. Then stir in the stock or water, add the soy sauce and the Worcestershire sauce and season. Bring to the boil then simmer, uncovered, for 5 minutes.

❺ Spoon into a medium-size pie dish, cover with the potato and smooth with the back of a fork. Scatter over the breadcrumbs. Bake for 25–30 minutes until the top is golden brown and the filling is cooked. Allow to stand for 10 minutes before serving as it will be very hot.

You can now find minced meat with very little fat. Look out for lean or extra lean varieties and check packs for details – they will often carry an eye-catching 'flash' giving you fat contents. To reduce the amount of fat in minced meat even more, simply dry-fry the meat in a heated, non-stick pan and drain off any fat.

Warming Winter Casserole

This is a complete meal in itself. There is no need to pre-fry the meat or vegetables, which makes this casserole even more healthy. Also, it is an ideal candidate for freezing, should you have any left over. Serve with cooked green cabbage or brussels sprouts, topped with a little grated nutmeg.

Serves: 4

Preparation time: 30 minutes + 1½ hours cooking

Freezing: recommended

Points per serving: with butter beans 5½; with kidney beans 6

Total Points per recipe: with butter beans 22; with kidney beans 24

Calories per serving: 370

480 g (1 lb) braising steak, trimmed of all fat and cut into 2 cm (¾-inch) cubes

2 lean-back bacon rashers, rind removed and chopped

1 onion, sliced thinly

2 celery sticks, sliced thinly

½ small swede, peeled and chopped

2 carrots, peeled and chopped

300 g (10 oz) potatoes, scrubbed and cut into chunks

240 g (8 oz) large button mushrooms, halved

210 g (7 oz) can butter beans or red kidney beans, drained

150 ml (¼ pint) dry cider or apple juice (optional)

600 ml (1 pint) beef stock

1 teaspoon ground cinnamon

1 teaspoon ground nutmeg

1 teaspoon garlic salt

1 teaspoon dried thyme

2 bay leaves

2 tablespoons chutney

2 tablespoons soy sauce

1 tablespoon cornflour

salt and freshly ground black pepper

1 Preheat the oven to Gas Mark 3/170°C/320°F. Simply put everything except the cornflour into a large flameproof casserole dish and season. On top of the stove, bring the casserole slowly to the boil, stirring occasionally.

2 Boil gently for 5 minutes, then cover and place in the oven to cook for about 1½ hours, or until the meat is tender.

3 Remove from the oven. Mix the cornflour with a little cold water and then stir briskly into the casserole. Stir over a gentle heat until thickened. Serve.

Many cuts of meat are now prepared by butchers to be as lean and as low in fat and saturated fat as possible. If there is any fat, you can cut it off before or after cooking.

Stuffed Pancakes with Mince and Lentils

Pancakes stuffed with lean mince make a wonderful supper dish. Serve either as a light meal with salad or as a satisfying main course with a selection of hot vegetables. This dish is also ideal for freezing, so feel free to make double the quantity and freeze half for later. If you wish, trickle a tablespoon of low-fat fromage frais over each serving of two pancakes. This will add 1 Point per serving and 10 Calories per serving.

Serves: 4

Preparation and cooking time: 35 minutes

Freezing: recommended

Points per serving: with beef 5; with pork 5; with lamb 5¹/₂

Total Points per recipe: with beef 20; with pork 20; with lamb 22

Calories per serving: with beef 310; with pork 305; with lamb 320

For the pancakes:
120 g (4 oz) plain flour
a good pinch of salt
1 egg
150 ml (¹/₄ pint) skimmed milk

150 ml (¹/₄ pint) water
low-fat cooking spray
For the filling:
240 g (8 oz) extra-lean minced beef, or minced pork or lamb
1 small onion, chopped
¹/₂ green pepper, chopped finely
1 garlic clove, crushed or 1 teaspoon garlic purée
3 tablespoons red lentils
420 g can chopped tomatoes
1 teaspoon dried oregano or marjoram
150 ml (¹/₄ pint) stock or water
salt and freshly ground black pepper
a little chopped fresh parsley, to serve

❶ Make the pancake batter by whizzing the flour, salt, egg, milk and water together in a food processor or blender. If making by hand, then gradually whisk the egg, milk and water into the flour and salt until you have a smooth batter.

❷ Heat a small heavy-based frying-pan, preferably non-stick, until you can feel a good steady heat rising. Spray lightly with low-fat cooking spray and pour in about 2 tablespoons of the batter, swirling the pan quickly so the mixture coats the base.

❸ Cook until the batter firms to a pancake and little holes appear. Loosen with a palette knife and flip over to cook the other side briefly. Slide the cooked pancake out and place in a clean tea towel.

❹ Repeat with the remaining mixture, reheating the pan in between each pancake and stacking the pancakes in the tea towel. You should have enough for 8 pancakes. Any extra ones can be frozen.

❺ To make the filling, heat another frying-pan until quite hot and spray with the cooking spray. Dry-fry the mince, stirring well to break up any lumps, then add the onion, pepper and garlic. Cook for about 5 minutes.

❻ Stir in the lentils, tomatoes, herbs and stock or water and seasoning. Bring to the boil, and then cover and simmer gently for 15 minutes until the mixture thickens and the lentils soften.

❼ Divide the filling between the eight pancakes and roll up. Arrange on a serving dish. Garnish with parsley and serve hot.

Country Cottage Pie (page 34)
Warming Winter Casserole (page 35)

Thai-Style Pot-Roast Pork

Thai food is increasingly popular, and many of the spicy ingredients are now readily available in supermarkets.
For this dish, a lean joint of pork is marinated and then cooked slowly in the oven until meltingly tender. Serve with rice
(ideally the fragrant and lightly sticky Thai rice) or boiled potatoes and a salad. If there is still a little fat on your joint
when you roast it, do be sure to cut it off at the table!

Serves: 6

Preparation time: 10 minutes + marinating
overnight + $1^{1}/_{2}$ hours roasting

Freezing: recommended

Points per serving: $6^{1}/_{2}$

Total Points per recipe: 39

Calories per serving: 240

1.05 kg ($2^{1}/_{4}$ lb) boned and rolled shoulder of
lean pork
2 teaspoons cornflour

For the paste:

2 plump fresh green chillies
1 onion, chopped
2 garlic cloves, crushed or 2 teaspoons garlic purée
1 small stem fresh lemon grass, chopped or the
grated rind of 1 lemon
2 teaspoons ginger purée
1 teaspoon freshly ground black pepper
2 teaspoons ground coriander
1 teaspoon ground cumin
3 tablespoons light soy sauce
1 tablespoon fresh lemon juice

❶ Untie the pork joint and slice off the rind and fat so it is nice and lean.

❷ Make the paste. Slit the chillies and scoop out the seeds (take care not to rub your eyes with your fingers afterwards, as the juice can sting). Chop the flesh roughly.

❸ Put the chillies into a food processor or blender together with the onion, garlic, lemon grass (or lemon rind), ginger purée, spices, 2 tablespoons soy sauce and lemon juice. Blend to a smooth paste scraping down the sides once.

❹ Spread some of this paste on the unrolled pork, then roll it up again and re-tie quite firmly.

❺ Place the pork on a large sheet of foil and spread the remaining paste over it. Scrunch up the foil fairly loosely, making sure the edges are well-sealed. Leave to marinate in the fridge for at least 2 hours, preferably overnight.

❻ Preheat the oven to Gas Mark 4/180°C/350°F. Place the foil parcel on a roasting pan and cook for about $1^{1}/_{2}$ hours until the meat is very tender. Uncover for the last half hour so the top browns.

❼ Remove the meat and leave to stand for 10 minutes before carving. Meanwhile add the remaining soy sauce to the meat juices in the roasting-pan. Heat on top of the stove, stirring well, until it boils. Blend the cornflour with a little cold water and whisk into the simmering pan juices. Strain into a jug and serve as a light sauce, allowing a tablespoon of sauce for each serving.

Cook's note: when cooking pork, for medium-cooked meat allow 30 minutes per 480 g (1 lb) plus 30 minutes; for well-done meat allow 35 minutes per 480 g (1 lb) plus 35 minutes.

Boned and rolled 'mini' joints need less cooking time and give an easy-to-carve joint.

Stuffed Pancakes with Mince and Lentils (page 36)
Sausage and Pepper Goulash (page 40)

Sausage and Pepper Goulash

Low-fat sausages are made from lean cuts of pork and each thick sausage has only 100 Calories. This recipe is a Hungarian-style casserole flavoured with peppers, tomatoes and paprika. Serve with mashed potatoes and whole green beans (remember to add the Points for the potato).

Serves: 4

Preparation and cooking time: 30 minutes

Freezing: recommended

Points per serving: 4¹/₂

Total Points per recipe: 18

Calories per serving: 305

8 thick low-fat pork sausages

1 large onion, sliced thinly

2 garlic cloves, crushed

1 red, green or yellow pepper, de-seeded and
  sliced thinly

1 tablespoon ground paprika

1 teaspoon dried mixed herbs

1 tablespoon wine vinegar

60 g (2 oz) macaroni

420 g can chopped tomatoes

300 ml (¹/₂ pint) stock or water

salt and freshly ground black pepper

To serve:

200 g carton 0%-fat fromage frais

chopped fresh parsley

❶ Cut each sausage in four. Preheat a non-stick frying pan until quite hot and dry-fry the sausage pieces until browned. Remove and set aside.

❷ Add the onion, garlic and pepper slices to the pan, together with 3 tablespoons of water. Cook, uncovered, until softened, about 5 minutes.

❸ Return the sausages to the pan. Stir in the paprika, dried mixed herbs and vinegar. Cook for about half a minute, then add the macaroni, tomatoes, stock (or water) and seasoning. Bring to the boil, then cover and simmer for 20 minutes, stirring once or twice. Allow to stand for 5 minutes before serving topped with fromage frais and a little chopped parsley.

Greek Stuffed Tomatoes

Capture the flavours of the Mediterranean with these colourful stuffed tomatoes. You will need large 'beef' tomatoes, and to speed up the cooking, it helps to cook the filling lightly before adding it to the tomatoes.

Serves: 4

Preparation time: 25 minutes + 20 minutes cooking

Freezing: not recommended

Points per serving: with beef 4; with pork 4;
  with lamb 4¹/₂

Total Points per recipe: with beef 16; with pork 16;
  with lamb 18

Calories per serving: with beef 255; with pork 250;
  with lamb 270

240 g (8 oz) extra-lean minced beef or minced
  pork or lamb

2 garlic cloves, crushed or 2 teaspoons garlic
  purée

¹/₂ small green pepper, chopped

1 carrot, grated coarsely

120 g (4 oz) risotto or long-grain rice (not easy-
  cook rice)

210 ml (7 fl oz) stock or water

1 teaspoon dried mixed herbs or oregano

4 large beef tomatoes

4 teaspoons low-fat natural yogurt

salt and freshly ground black pepper

❶ Heat a frying-pan until quite hot and dry-fry the mince until browned and crumbly. Add the garlic, green pepper and carrot. Cook for another 5 minutes.
❷ Stir in the rice, stock (or water), herbs and seasoning. Bring to the boil, then cover. Turn down the heat and simmer for 15 minutes.
❸ Meanwhile, slice the tops off the tomatoes and put aside. Scoop out the flesh using a small sharp knife and teaspoon. Chop the tomato flesh roughly and add to the rice and mince.

❹ When the filling mixture is just-cooked and the liquid has been absorbed, spoon into the tomato shells and cover with the tops.
❺ Heat the oven to Gas Mark 5/190°C/375°F. Place the tomatoes in a shallow ovenproof dish and bake for 20–25 minutes until softened but still holding a good shape. Cool slightly before serving. Top with a small spoonful of natural yogurt.

Ham and Pea Risotto

A classic Italian dish which is deliciously satisfying, and easy to make. Ideally, use a risotto rice: the starchy grains produce a rich creaminess without adding extra Points or Calories

Serves: 4
Preparation and cooking time: 25 minutes
Freezing: not recommended
Points per serving: 7½
Total Points per recipe: 30
Calories per serving: 440

1 onion, chopped
2 garlic cloves, crushed or 1 teaspoon garlic
    purée

2 teaspoons olive oil
300 g (10 oz) risotto rice, e.g. arborio or carnaroli
    or long-grain rice (but not easy-cook rice)
3 tablespoons dry vermouth or white wine
    (optional)
1.2 litres (2 pints) stock
240 g (8 oz) lean ham, chopped
240 g (8 oz) peas, thawed if frozen
30 g (1 oz) fresh parmesan cheese, grated
salt and freshly ground black pepper

❶ Put the onion, garlic, oil and 2 tablespoons of water in a medium-size saucepan. Heat until sizzling, then cover tightly and cook gently for 5 minutes.
❷ Stir in the rice and cook for a minute. Then add the vermouth or wine (if using) and cook until all the alcohol has evaporated.
❸ Stir in a quarter of the stock. Bring to the boil and simmer, uncovered, until it has been absorbed.

Now, gradually stir in the remaining stock in stages – about a quarter at a time. Wait until each amount of stock has been absorbed before adding some more. Stir frequently in between.
❹ Add the ham and peas and simmer for another 3 minutes. Season well. The mixture should be nice and creamy and the rice just cooked. Serve immediately sprinkled with the parmesan cheese.

Meatloaf with Fresh Tomato Salsa

Mixing beef and pork is an Italian idea and one that works really well in this quick meatloaf. Serve it hot as a midweek 'roast' with pasta, rice or mashed potatoes, or cold with a salad and baked potatoes. The salsa makes a fresh and exotic accompaniment, but this loaf could also be served with a spoonful or two of ready-made pasta sauce.

Serves: 6

Preparation time: 15 minutes + 40 minutes cooking

Freezing: recommended for meatloaf only

Points per serving: 3

Total Points per recipe: 18

Calories per serving: 175

240 g (8 oz) extra-lean beef mince

240 g (8 oz) pork mince

2 tablespoons soy sauce

1 tablespoon Worcestershire sauce

1 teaspoon garlic salt

1 teaspoon salt

2 teaspoons dried mixed herbs or oregano

1 large egg

low-fat cooking spray

freshly ground black pepper

For the salsa:

4 medium tomatoes

$^1/_2$ red pepper, de-seeded

$^1/_2$ small onion

1 tablespoon fresh parsley, chopped

1 tablespoon fresh lemon juice

1 teaspoon mild chilli powder

$^1/_2$ teaspoon ground cumin (optional)

salt and freshly ground black pepper

❶ Mix the two minces together until thoroughly blended (this is best done with clean hands), then beat in the soy sauce and Worcestershire sauce, garlic salt, salt, herbs, egg and pepper.

❷ Line a 480 g (1 lb) loaf tin with foil and spray lightly with low-fat cooking spray. Press the mince mixture into the tin.

❸ Preheat the oven to Gas Mark 5/190°C/375°F. Bake the loaf for about 40 minutes until it feels quite firm. Remove from the oven and allow to stand for 10 minutes before draining off the meat juices.

❹ While the loaf is cooking, make the salsa. To skin the tomatoes, place them in boiling water for a minute or two, and then dip them into cold water. Peel off the skins and chop the flesh finely.

❺ Grate the pepper and onion on a coarse grater and mix with the tomato, parsley, lemon juice, chilli powder, cumin (if using) and seasoning. The salsa is now ready. Serve the loaf cut in slices with the salsa.

Special Spinach Lasagne

A home-made lasagne is always welcome and quite easy to put together. Add a little colour and texture with some chopped leaf spinach and top with a quick all-in-one white sauce. Serve with a green salad or some green beans.

Serves: 4

Preparation and cooking time: 20 minutes + 45 minutes cooking

Freezing: recommended

Points per serving: with beef 7½; with pork 7; with lamb 8½

Total Points per recipe: with beef 30; with pork 28; with lamb 34

Calories per serving: with beef 465; with pork 455; with lamb 490

480 g (1 lb) extra-lean minced beef, or minced pork or lamb

1 onion, chopped

2 garlic cloves, crushed

2 tablespoons red wine (optional)

420 g can chopped tomatoes

2 tablespoons tomato purée

1 teaspoon dried oregano

200 g bag fresh leaf spinach

6 sheets no pre-cook lasagne

2 tablespoons freshly grated parmesan cheese

salt and freshly ground black pepper

For the white sauce:

420 ml (14 fl oz) skimmed milk

00 g (1 oz) plain flour

30 g (1 oz) low-fat spread

½ teaspoon ground nutmeg

1 Heat a non-stick frying-pan until quite hot. Dry-fry the mince until browned, stirring to break up the lumps.

2 Add the onion and garlic and cook for 5 minutes. Stir in the wine (if using), tomatoes, tomato purée, oregano and seasoning. Bring to the boil, then simmer for 10 minutes, stirring occasionally.

3 Chop the spinach and add to the mince sauce, stirring until wilted.

4 Make the white sauce by putting the milk, flour and low-fat spread into a saucepan. Bring to the boil, whisking until thickened and smooth. Season well and mix in the nutmeg.

5 Preheat the oven to Gas Mark 5/190°C/375°F. Put a layer of meat sauce in the base of a medium-size ovenproof casserole. Arrange pasta sheets on top, making sure none overlap, and breaking to fit if necessary. Pour over a third of the white sauce.

6 Repeat the layering of meat sauce, pasta and white sauce as above. Finish with a combination of white sauce and meat sauce lightly swirled together to give an attractive finish.

7 Sprinkle over the cheese and bake for about 30 minutes until golden brown and bubbling on top. Let the lasagne stand for about 10 minutes or more before serving.

Beef Topside with Roasted Vegetables

Joints of beef topside make good midweek meals and are ideal for all-in-one roasting with vegetables which creates a wonderful exchange of flavours. Serve the meat and vegetables, and any juices from the meat, along with some lightly boiled green leafy cabbage or your choice of 'greens'. If there is still a little fat on your joint when you roast it, do be sure to cut it off at the table!

Serves: 6

Preparation and cooking time: 10 minutes + 1½ hours roasting

Freezing: recommended for leftovers

Points per serving: 5½

Total Points per recipe: 33

Calories per serving: 315

1.05 kg (2¼ lb 4 oz) lean beef topside
3 potatoes, scrubbed

3 carrots, peeled
3 parsnips, peeled
1 onion, cut in thick chunks
1 red, green or yellow pepper, de-seeded and cut in thick chunks
2 celery sticks, sliced thickly
1 teaspoon dried thyme
1 tablespoon olive or sunflower oil
salt and freshly ground black pepper

❶ Trim the topside of any fat and re-tie with string. Preheat the oven to Gas Mark 4/180°C/350°F.

❷ Cut the potatoes, carrots and parsnips into big chunks of equal sizes and pop them into a polythene food bag with the other vegetables. Sprinkle in lots of seasoning together with the thyme and shake the bag well.

❸ Pour in the oil and rub it into all the vegetables shaking the bag occasionally. Tip the vegetables into the roasting pan, pour in 450 ml (¾ pint) of water, and put the joint on top.

❹ Roast for 1½ hours for medium beef and 1 hour 40 minutes for well-done beef (see Cook's note).

❺ Remove the pan from the oven and allow to stand undisturbed for 10 minutes. Take out the beef and cut into thin slices with a sharp carving knife. Serve with the vegetables and any pan juices.

Cook's note: when cooking beef, for rare meat allow 20 minutes per 480 g (1 lb) plus 20 minutes; for medium-cooked meat allow 25 minutes per 480 g (1 lb) plus 25 minutes; for well-done meat allow 30 minutes per 480 g (1 lb) plus 30 minutes.

Roasted meats should be allowed to stand for about 10 minutes after cooking. This helps make carving easy and allows juices to be absorbed back into the meat, giving you a juicier joint. Don't worry, your joint won't lose much heat.

Beef Topside with Roasted Vegetables
Greek Stuffed Tomatoes (page 40)

Barbecue-Style Tandoori Lamb

Traditional tandoori cooking uses a hot clay oven which cooks lean meat at a very high temperature for a short time, keeping the meat moist and tender. You can imitate this cooking style at home by marinating the meat first in a spicy, low-fat natural yogurt marinade and then cooking it at a high temperature. For the traditional tandoori red colour, use a few drops of edible red and yellow food colourings, otherwise leave it looking wholesome and natural.

Serves: 4

Preparation and cooking time: 30 minutes + marinating time

Freezing: recommended

Points per serving: 5¹/₂

Total Points per recipe: 22

Calories per serving: 450

4 × 120 g (4 oz) boneless lamb leg steaks, trimmed of all fat

fresh lemon juice

salt

For the marinade:

210 ml (7 fl oz) low-fat natural yogurt

¹/₂ **small onion, grated**

2 garlic cloves, crushed

2 teaspoons ginger purée

1 small mild green chilli, chopped finely

2 teaspoons mild curry powder or garam masala powder

¹/₂ teaspoon ground turmeric

2 teaspoons ground paprika

To serve:

4 medium wholemeal pitta breads

crisp green salad leaves

1 lemon, quartered

❶ Season the lamb well and sprinkle with lemon juice. Set aside for 5 minutes while you make the marinade.

❷ Mix the yogurt with the rest of the marinade ingredients, then pour into a food bag. Add the lamb steaks and rub the marinade in well. Seal and chill for at least 2 hours, but preferably overnight.

❸ Preheat the oven to Gas Mark 8/230°C/450°F. Set a grill rack over a small roasting pan. Remove the lamb from the marinade, and place on the rack.

❹ Cook in the hot oven for 20–25 minutes according to how you like your lamb cooked – medium or well-done. Allow to stand for 5 minutes. Season lightly, then slice and serve tucked inside the pitta breads. Add the crisp salad leaves and serve with lemon quarters.

Index